Straight Forward with Science

The
Human
Body

Peter Riley

W

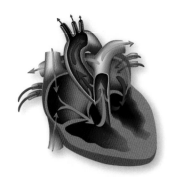

To my granddaughter, Tabitha Grace.

Published in paperback in Great Britain in 2018 by The Watts Publishing Group

Editor: Julia Bird
Designer: Mo Choy

ISBN: 978 1 4451 3543 4
Library ebook ISBN 978 1 4451 3542 7
Dewey classification number: 599

Photo acknowledgments: Africa Studio/Shutterstock: 23tl. Alila Medical Media/Shutterstock: 9t. Biofoto Associates/SPL: 19t. Jose Luis Calvo/Shutterstock: 3, 7b. Scott Camazine/Alamy: 29tl. chanawitsitthisombat/Alamy: 9b. Valentyna Chukhlyebova/Shutterstock: 5b. Matthew Cole/Shutterstock: 8b. Frederic Legrand-Comeo/Shutterstock: 25t. Henning Dalhoff/SPL: 10. Emin Dzkam/Shutterstock: 23tr. Everett Collection/Alamy: 28b. Everett Historical/Shutterstock: 28t. Evgeniash/Shutterstock: 18t. Steve Gschmeissner/SPL/Alamy: 17t. Levente Gyon/Shutterstock: 11b. hartphotography/Shutterstock: 21t. ifong/Shutterstock: 19b. Isarescheewin/Shutterstock: 16tr. Sebastien Kaulitzki/Shutterstock: 5tr. Alain Lauga/Dreamstime:15tr. Lighthunter/Shutterstock: 27t. martan/Shutterstock: 7t.Monkey Business Images/Shutterstock: 26t. Motovolka/Shutterstock: 26b. murengstockphoto/Shutterstock: 22. National Cancer Institute/SPL: 13r, 31. Ninell/Shutterstock: 5tl. Nixx Photography/Shutterstock: 12. North Wind P A/Alamy: 29b. Peerayot/Shutterstock: 21b. Phanie/Alamy: 8t. Photosky/Shutterstock: 27b. S Pytel/Shutterstock: front cover, 1. Eunita R/Shutterstock: 15bl. Gunita R/Shutterstock: 16bl. Antonio S/Shutterstock: 18c. Doug Shutter/Shutterstock: 23br. Somchai Som/Shutterstock: 23tc. SPL/Alamy: 4. Marmaduke St John/Alamy: 23cl. Suzanne Tucker/Shutterstock: 13l, 24. URRA/Shutterstock: 14. Jun Wat/Shutterstock: 18b. XiXinXing/Shutterstock: 11t.

Printed in China

Franklin Watts
An imprint of
Hachette Children's Group
Part of The Watts Publishing Group
Carmelite House
50 Victoria Embankment1
London EC4Y 0DZ

An Hachette UK Company
www.hachette.co.uk

www.franklinwatts.co.uk

FSC
www.fsc.org
MIX
Paper from
responsible sources
FSC® C104740

Contents

Organs

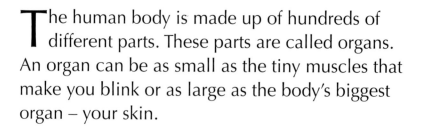

The human body is made up of hundreds of different parts. These parts are called organs. An organ can be as small as the tiny muscles that make you blink or as large as the body's biggest organ – your skin.

WORKING TOGETHER

Each organ does not work alone. It works in a group with other similar organs. These groups of organs are called organ systems. There are eleven organ systems in the human body.

The respiratory system is made up of the windpipe, lungs and chest. They work together to take in oxygen and release carbon dioxide.

The digestive system is a very long tube running through the body. It breaks down food so that it can be taken into the blood.

The excretory system is made up of the kidneys and bladder. It gets rid of liquid waste from the body.

The circulatory system is made up of the heart, blood vessels and blood. It carries a wide range of substances around the body to where they are needed.

The skeletal system is made up of bones. It gives the body support, protects many other organs and, through the joints between the bones, allows the body to move.

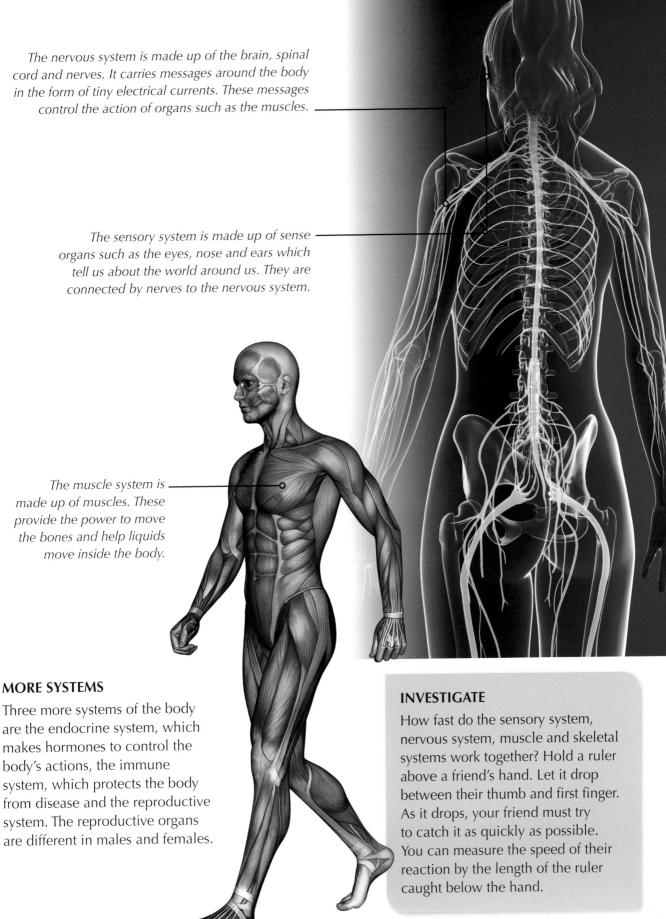

The nervous system is made up of the brain, spinal cord and nerves. It carries messages around the body in the form of tiny electrical currents. These messages control the action of organs such as the muscles.

The sensory system is made up of sense organs such as the eyes, nose and ears which tell us about the world around us. They are connected by nerves to the nervous system.

The muscle system is made up of muscles. These provide the power to move the bones and help liquids move inside the body.

MORE SYSTEMS

Three more systems of the body are the endocrine system, which makes hormones to control the body's actions, the immune system, which protects the body from disease and the reproductive system. The reproductive organs are different in males and females.

INVESTIGATE

How fast do the sensory system, nervous system, muscle and skeletal systems work together? Hold a ruler above a friend's hand. Let it drop between their thumb and first finger. As it drops, your friend must try to catch it as quickly as possible. You can measure the speed of their reaction by the length of the ruler caught below the hand.

5

Cells

The organs are made up of tiny parts called cells. Cells are often described as the building blocks of the body. Just as a house is made up of individual bricks, a body is made up of individual cells.

MICROSCOPIC CELLS

Scientists have estimated that the human body is made up of up to 37 trillion cells. Cells can only be seen with a microscope. They are so small that about 200 cells would fit on the full stop at the end of this sentence!

PARTS OF A CELL

An animal cell has three main parts. At its centre is a ball-shaped structure called the nucleus, which contains deoxyribonucleic acid (DNA). DNA has the instructions for making all the parts of the cell and making the cell perform its task in the life of the body. Around the nucleus is a semi-liquid substance like runny jelly called cytoplasm. It contains many tiny structures which work together to keep the cell alive. The third part is the cell membrane. This is like a thin skin around the cell, which holds in the other parts. It has tiny holes in it which let substances such as digested food and oxygen into the cell and give out waste in the form of carbon dioxide.

❙ The three main parts of an animal cell.

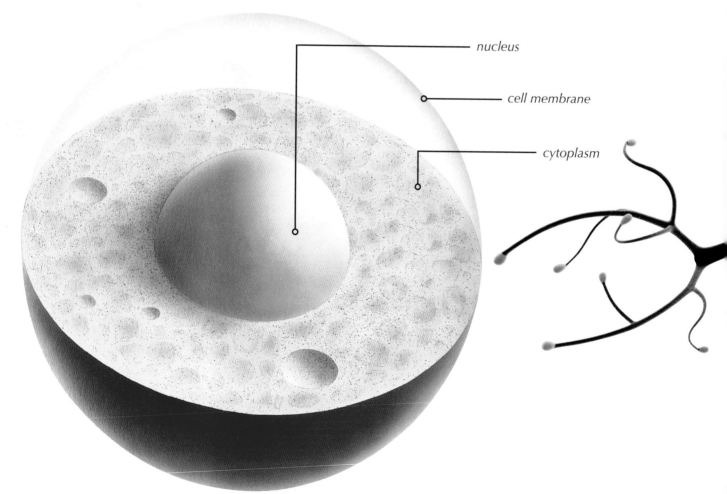

nucleus

cell membrane

cytoplasm

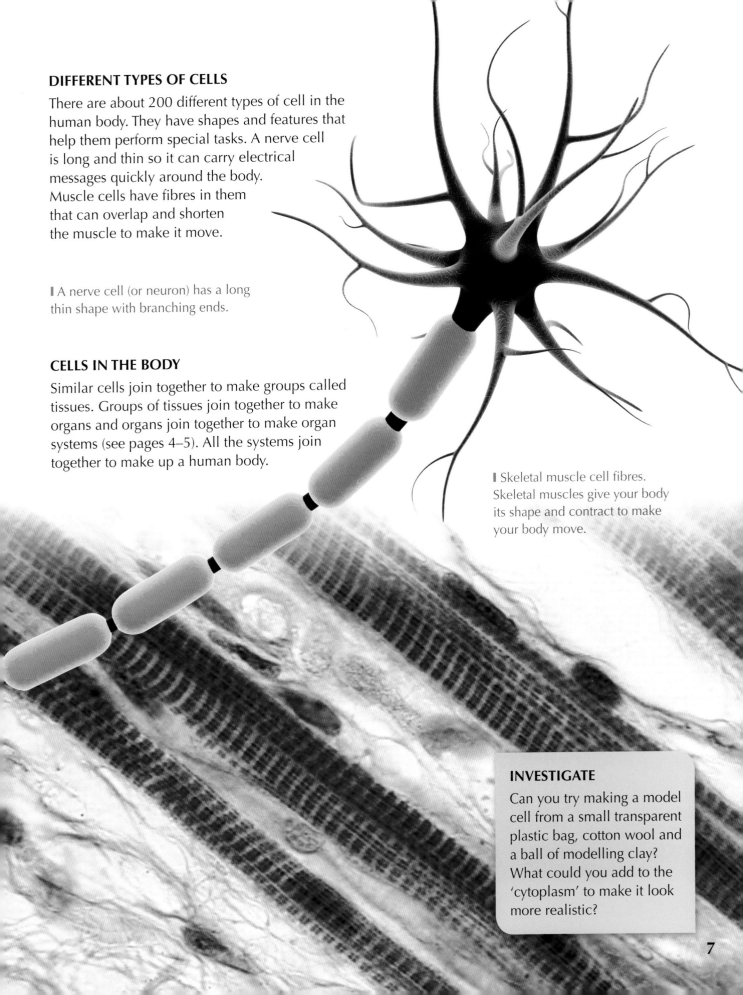

DIFFERENT TYPES OF CELLS

There are about 200 different types of cell in the human body. They have shapes and features that help them perform special tasks. A nerve cell is long and thin so it can carry electrical messages quickly around the body. Muscle cells have fibres in them that can overlap and shorten the muscle to make it move.

❙ A nerve cell (or neuron) has a long thin shape with branching ends.

CELLS IN THE BODY

Similar cells join together to make groups called tissues. Groups of tissues join together to make organs and organs join together to make organ systems (see pages 4–5). All the systems join together to make up a human body.

❙ Skeletal muscle cell fibres. Skeletal muscles give your body its shape and contract to make your body move.

INVESTIGATE

Can you try making a model cell from a small transparent plastic bag, cotton wool and a ball of modelling clay? What could you add to the 'cytoplasm' to make it look more realistic?

The heart

The heart is at the centre of the circulatory system (see pages 14–15). It is about the size of your clenched fist and is located slightly to the left of your chest. It is made of muscle cells in the form of fibres. These fibres shorten and lengthen to make your heart beat.

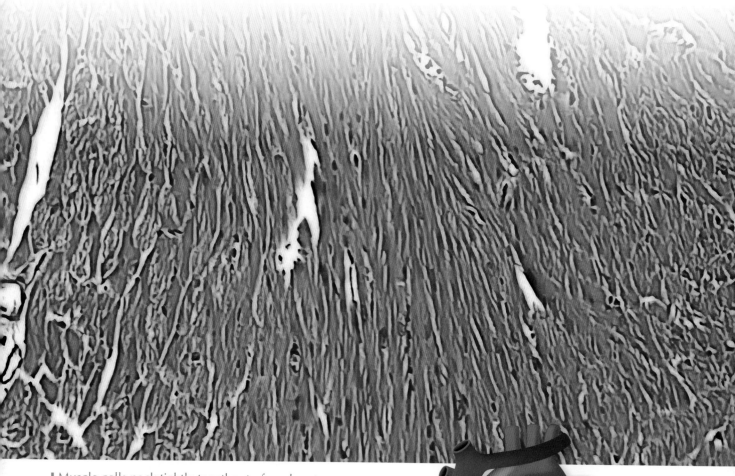

▌Muscle cells pack tightly together to form heart muscle tissue.

PARTS OF THE HEART

There is a muscular wall down the middle of the heart which divides it into a right side and a left side. The right side is divided into two cavities or chambers which hold the blood. The top chamber is called the right atrium. The bottom chamber is called the right ventricle. The two chambers are separated by the tricuspid valve. The left side is also divided into two cavities – the left atrium and the left ventricle. They are separated by the bicuspid valve.

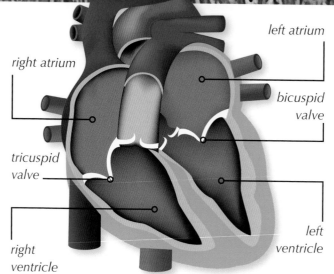

right atrium

left atrium

bicuspid valve

tricuspid valve

right ventricle

left ventricle

THE PATH OF BLOOD THROUGH THE HEART

There are a group of blood vessels attached to the top of the heart. They carry blood to and from the heart. On the right side of the heart is a large vein called the vena cava. It brings blood from the body into the right atrium. Blood passes from here through the tricuspid valve into the right ventricle. It then travels through the semi-lunar valve into the pulmonary artery, which carries the blood to the lungs.

On the left side of the heart, the pulmonary veins bring blood from the lungs into the left atrium. The blood passes through the left atrium through the bicuspid valve into the left ventricle. It then travels through the semi-lunar valve into an artery called the aorta. From here, the blood travels all around the body.

❚ Parts of the heart can be faulty or become damaged over time. They can sometimes be repaired with surgery.

INVESTIGATE

Make a model of the heart using modelling clay. Use blue and red pipe cleaners to show the path of blood through the heart.

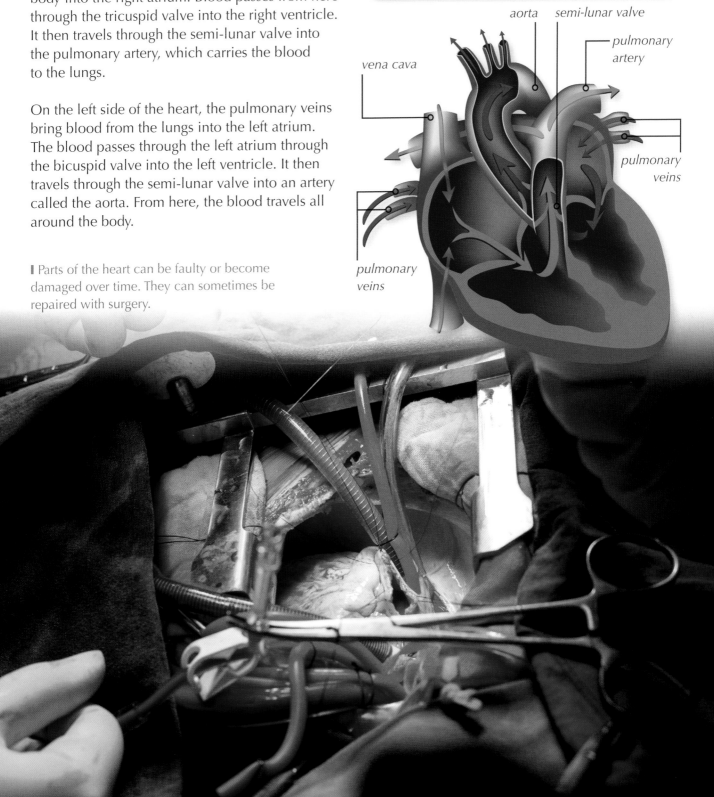

aorta

semi-lunar valve

pulmonary artery

vena cava

pulmonary veins

pulmonary veins

The heart in action

The right and left sides of the heart are pumps. They take in blood and pump it out. The power of the heart pumps the blood all the way around the body.

PUMP ACTION

The pump action begins when blood enters an atrium. The muscles in the atrium wall make it push on the blood and force it through the valve into the ventricle. The bicuspid or tricuspid valve closes behind the blood to stop it going back. Muscles in the ventricle wall make it push on the blood and force it through the semi-lunar valves and out of the heart. The semi-lunar valves close behind it and stop it going backwards. Both sides of the heart work in the same way at the same time. This means that both atria fill at the same time, both the biscuspid and tricuspid valves shut at the same time, both ventricles empty at the same time and both semi-lunar valves shut at the same time.

I The ventricles begin to squeeze the blood and direct it towards the semi-lunar valves as the the bicuspid or tricuspid valves start to close.

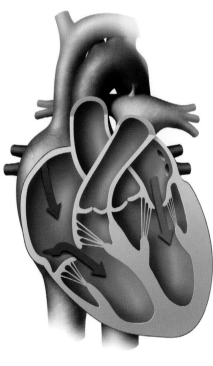

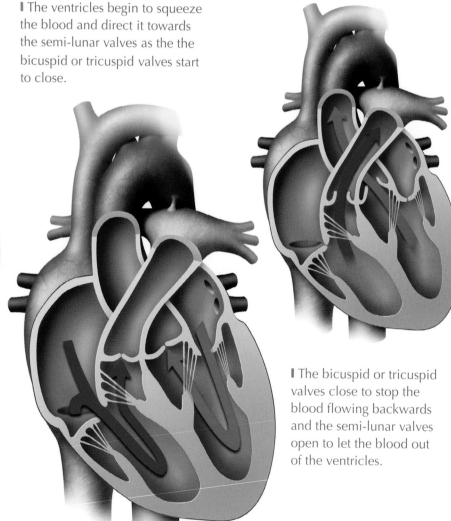

I First, blood moves from the atria to the ventricles.

I The bicuspid or tricuspid valves close to stop the blood flowing backwards and the semi-lunar valves open to let the blood out of the ventricles.

HEART SOUNDS

When doctors check the health of the heart, they use a stethoscope and listen to the sounds the heart is making. When the tricuspid and bicuspid valves close together they make a 'lub' sound. When the two semi-lunar valves close together they make a 'dup' sound. The sound of the valves closing after each other is 'lub dup'.

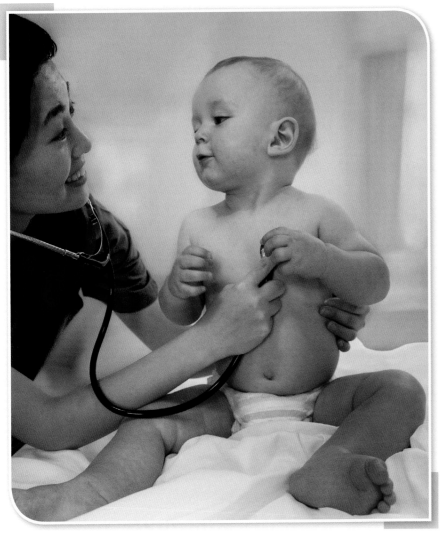

❚ Over this baby's lifetime, his heart will beat over two billion times!

THE PULSE

Blood leaving the heart moves along blood vessels called arteries. The pumping action of the heart makes the walls of the arteries expand and contract as the blood passes along them. This movement of the artery wall can be felt as a throbbing sensation by the fingers. It is called the pulse and throbs at the same speed as the heart beats. Doctors also use this when checking the health of the heart. Your pulse can be felt in your wrist or in your throat.

❚ The radial artery passes under your wrist. It expands as blood passes through it and this is what you can feel as your pulse.

INVESTIGATE

Take your pulse by placing your fingers as shown in the picture. You may have to move your fingers around a little to find your pulse. How many times does your heart beat in a minute?

The blood

Blood is a mixture of blood cells and a watery liquid called plasma. The red blood cells give blood its colour.

PLASMA

Plasma makes up just over half the volume of a drop of blood. It is pale yellow, but its colour cannot be seen because of the red blood cells that are mixed with it. Plasma has many substances dissolved in it. These include digested proteins, carbohydrates and fats, vitamins and minerals. It also contains two of the body's waste products. These are carbon dioxide, which is produced by all of the body's cells and a substance called urea. Urea is made in the liver when too much protein (see page 18) has been eaten for the body to use. It is also made in the tissues when the cells repair themselves after being damaged.

RED BLOOD CELLS

There are about five million red blood cells in just one drop of blood measuring one millimetre across! The bones of the ribs, breastbone and backbone make over a million red blood cells a second and they travel round the blood for about four months before they wear out and are destroyed in the liver. Each cell is packed with a protein called haemoglobin. When the red cells pass through the lungs, the haemoglobin picks up oxygen and the blood becomes bright red or oxygenated. As the blood goes around other parts of the body the haemoglobin passes the oxygen to the cells and the blood becomes darker or deoxygenated.

▌These two blood samples show plasma separated out from the rest of the blood (left); and blood mixed together (right).

WHITE BLOOD CELLS

There are about 800 times fewer white blood cells than red cells in a drop of blood. White blood cells work with the immune system to keep your body healthy. There are two main types. One type seeks out germs and eats them. The other makes substances called antibodies to protect the body from disease.

PLATELETS

There are twenty times fewer platelets than red cells in a drop of blood. Platelets are made from pieces of cells. When a blood vessel is cut and starts to bleed, platelets make a microscopic fibre netting across the wound. This forms a clot that stops the blood escaping from the body and seals it to prevent germs getting in.

❙ This highly magnified photo of blood (right) shows red blood cells (red), white blood cells (yellow) and platelets (pink).

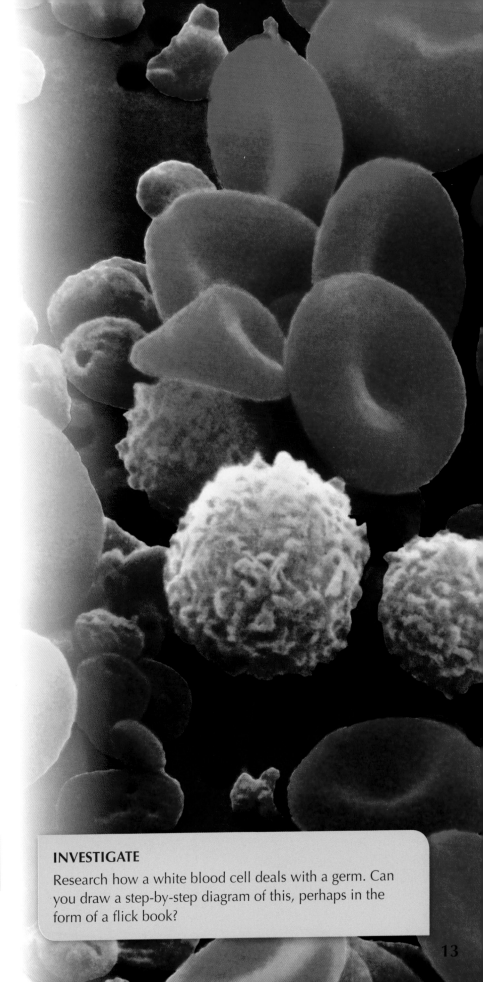

❙ A scab forms over a wound to protect the tissues underneath and help them heal.

INVESTIGATE

Research how a white blood cell deals with a germ. Can you draw a step-by-step diagram of this, perhaps in the form of a flick book?

The circulatory system

The circulatory system is composed of the heart and the blood vessels. It transports blood around the body. The cells in every organ take in dissolved nutrients from the blood. They take in oxygen from the red cells and use it to release energy from food to stay alive through respiration (see page 17). In this process they make carbon dioxide that passes into plasma and is carried away.

BLOOD VESSELS

There are three types of blood vessel. Arteries take blood away from the heart. Capillaries transport blood through every organ and veins bring blood back to the heart.

STRUCTURE

Arteries have thick, flexible walls that can withstand the powerful push of the blood as it leaves the heart. Capillaries are much finer than arteries. They have very thin walls so dissolved substances in the blood and cells can easily pass through them into the body. Veins are a similar size to the arteries but have much thinner walls as the push of the blood is much weaker here. They also have valves to stop the blood flowing backwards and keep it flowing towards the heart.

ARRANGEMENT

Arteries are usually buried deep in the body, while veins are found nearer the skin. You can probably see some under the skin in your wrist. This diagram shows how the arteries and veins are connected to the heart and the main organs.

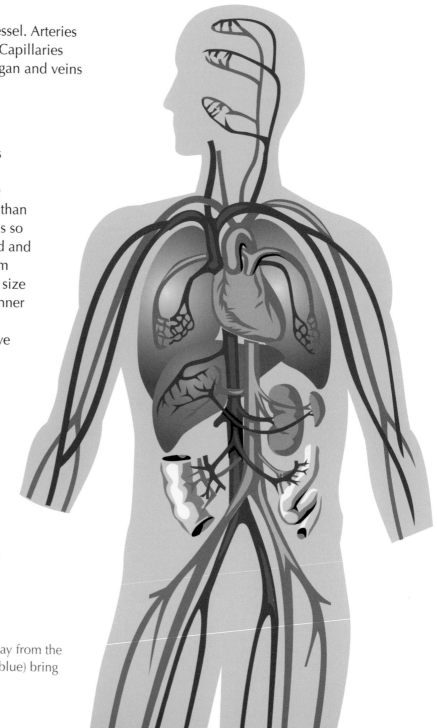

❚ The arteries (red) take the blood away from the heart to the body organs. The veins (blue) bring blood back to the heart.

BLOOD AND THE LUNGS

When an artery reaches an organ, it splits into a huge number of tiny capillaries. It is here that changes in the blood take place. In the lungs, oxygen from the air passes through the capillary walls and enters the red blood cells. Carbon dioxide dissolved in the plasma passes through the capillary wall to the lungs where it is then breathed out.

BLOOD AND THE KIDNEYS

The kidneys filter out toxins and waste products such as urea from the blood and return the filtered blood to circulate through the body. In the kidneys, urea dissolved in the plasma passes through the capillary wall and into tubes which lead to the bladder. Here it is stored as a watery liquid called urine before being eventually released from the body.

❙ The kidneys play a vital role in keeping your blood healthy.

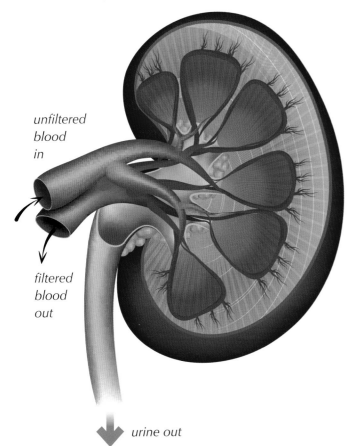

unfiltered
blood
in

filtered
blood
out

urine out

❙ These runners are breathing hard to exchange oxygen and carbon dioxide quickly as they use up energy in their food (see pages 16–17) to run up a hill.

INVESTIGATE

Blood flows at about 40cm per second in an artery. Use a tape measure to find out how long it takes to get from your heart to your big toe.

Digestion and respiration

The body of every living thing needs food to survive. Food provides materials called nutrients for the cells and energy for living processes, such as growth. Plants make their own food by photosynthesis using the energy in sunlight, water from the soil and carbon dioxide in the air. Animals cannot make their own food and so must get the nutrients and energy they need from the bodies of other living things.

▎These grass plants are making food from the energy in sunlight. Sheep eat the grass to get the nutrients they need to live.

DIGESTION

The nutrients in the cells of living things are arranged in a special way. When an animal eats these cells it cannot use the nutrients as they are arranged. They have to be taken apart first, just as you might take apart the pieces of a jigsaw. The body process which breaks up the nutrients in food is called digestion. It takes place in the digestive system (opposite). Juices like the saliva in your mouth are produced by organs of the digestive system. They contain substances called enzymes which break up the food into nutrients that the body can use.

ABSORPTION AND CIRCULATION

Once nutrients have been separated, they pass through the wall of the small intestine into the blood. From here they are moved round the body by the beating action of the heart. As blood moves through the capillaries in the body's organs, the nutrients pass through the capillary walls, the cell walls and into the cells where they are used to keep the cells alive.

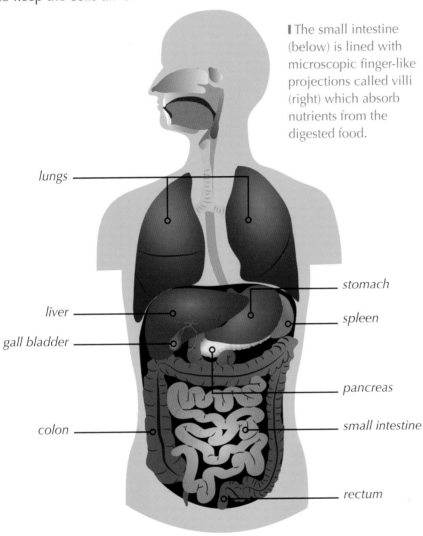

I The small intestine (below) is lined with microscopic finger-like projections called villi (right) which absorb nutrients from the digested food.

lungs

stomach

liver

spleen

gall bladder

pancreas

colon

small intestine

rectum

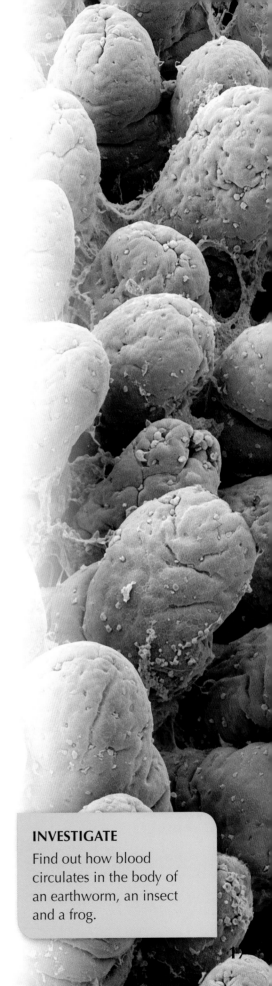

RESPIRATION

Inside a cell a process called respiration takes place. In this process energy is released from a nutrient called glucose. Oxygen is needed for the energy to be released. It comes from the air in the lungs and travels in the haemoglobin in red blood cells to the cells in an organ such as a muscle. During respiration, carbon dioxide is made. It passes out of the cell into the plasma and is taken away to the lungs where it is excreted into the air (see page 15). The energy released is used in many ways. It may be used to keep the cell warm, to send an electrical message in a nerve cell, make a muscle cell move or help a cell in the digestive system to produce an enzyme.

INVESTIGATE

Find out how blood circulates in the body of an earthworm, an insect and a frog.

Diet and health

Your diet is the food that you usually eat every week. It provides your body with nutrients and fibre. Your body requires certain amounts of each nutrient to keep healthy and grow properly. A balanced diet provides this.

▌Carbohydrate-rich foods are a good source of energy.

CARBOHYDRATES

Carbohydrates should make up a large part of your diet as they supply the body with energy that it can use straightaway. They are found in starchy foods, such as rice, bread, potatoes and pasta.

▌Oily fish such as mackerel is rich in protein and helps protect your heart.

PROTEINS

Proteins are the building materials of the body. They are used to make cells, for the growth of the body and for repairing injuries. They are found in meat, fish, beans, peas and lentils.

FATS

Fats provide the body with an energy store and provide an insulating layer under the skin to keep the body warm. They are found in butter, cream, cheese, nuts and some meats.

▌Leafy green vegetables are full of essential vitamins and minerals (see opposite).

VITAMINS AND MINERALS

Vitamins protect the body from disease and help the organs to work properly. They are found in fruit, vegetables and milk. Minerals are needed to make parts of the body. Iron is a mineral that makes haemoglobin and calcium is a mineral that makes up bone. Iron and calcium are found in many foods, including eggs, milk and cereals and leafy green vegetables such as spinach.

NUTRIENTS – TOO LITTLE ...

Malnutrition can occur when the body takes in too few or too many of certain nutrients. Too little iron in your diet, for example, can cause a blood disorder called anaemia. Too little vitamin D in your diet can cause a bone disease called rickets. Too little of all nutrients prevents the body from growing properly.

... AND TOO MUCH

Eating too much sugar causes bacteria to feed on it in the mouth. The bacteria produce acids that attack the teeth and cause decay. Sugar is also a form of carbohydrate. When you take in too much sugar, the body changes it into fat and stores it under the skin. Too much fat can also be stored in this way. The extra fat in your body can lead to a condition called obesity. In time, obesity can damage the circulatory system and heart, put pressure on your bones and joints and even lead to a blood sugar disorder called diabetes.

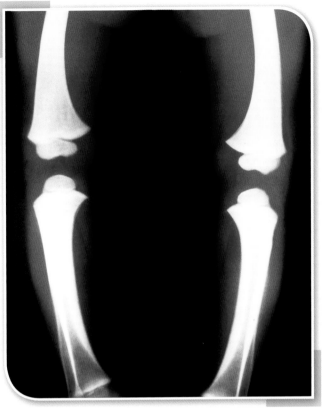

▍Rickets makes bones weak. It has made these leg bones bend because they are not strong enough to support the body.

INVESTIGATE

A food pyramid shows the amounts of food you should have in your diet – a few from the top and plenty from the bottom. Keep a record of what you eat in a week and match it to the pyramid. Is your diet balanced?

Fighting disease

Most diseases are caused by microorganisms that enter the body and breed there. The body has defences to attack them, but scientists have also developed vaccines and medicines to help prevent and cure disease.

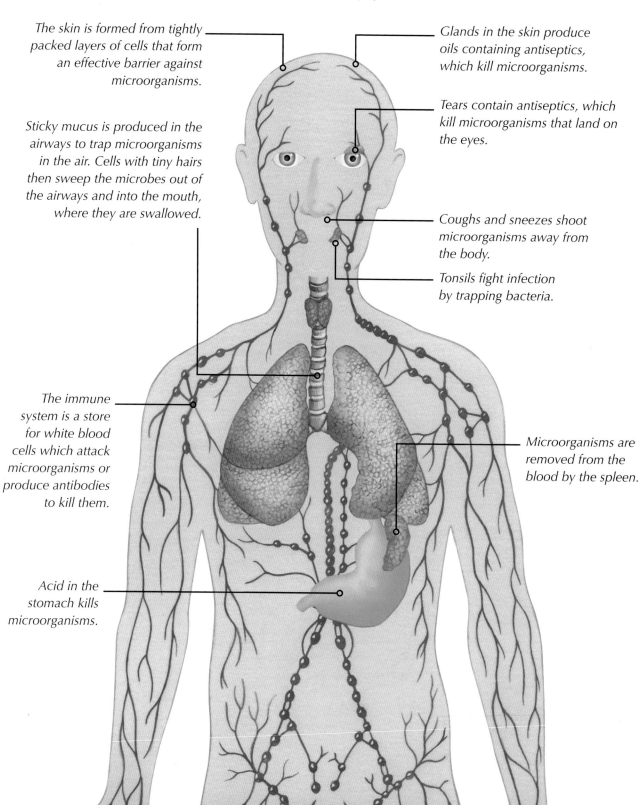

The skin is formed from tightly packed layers of cells that form an effective barrier against microorganisms.

Sticky mucus is produced in the airways to trap microorganisms in the air. Cells with tiny hairs then sweep the microbes out of the airways and into the mouth, where they are swallowed.

The immune system is a store for white blood cells which attack microorganisms or produce antibodies to kill them.

Acid in the stomach kills microorganisms.

Glands in the skin produce oils containing antiseptics, which kill microorganisms.

Tears contain antiseptics, which kill microorganisms that land on the eyes.

Coughs and sneezes shoot microorganisms away from the body.

Tonsils fight infection by trapping bacteria.

Microorganisms are removed from the blood by the spleen.

MICROORGANISM INVADERS

Microorganism invaders can come from three groups of living things – bacteria, Protoctista microbes and fungi, and one group of non-living things – viruses. Harmful bacteria can cause diseases such as cholera, typhoid and tuberculosis. Protoctista can cause malaria, while harmful fungi can cause infections in the mouth called thrush and skin infections such as athlete's foot. Viruses can cause many illnesses, including colds, influenza (flu) and chickenpox.

❚ Chickenpox is caused by the varicella-zoster virus and spreads very quickly, particularly among children.

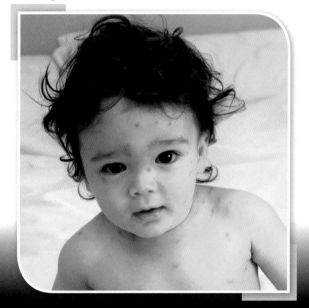

MEDICINES

Medicines are substances that help the body fight disease and help it recover full health. There is a group of medicines called medical or prescription drugs. Children must be given these by adult members of a family, carers or doctors and nurses. Only a certain amount of medicine is given at a time. This amount is called the dose. There is a certain time interval between taking doses such as once a day or every four hours. There is also a certain number of doses that can be taken and this is called a course of medication.

VACCINES

A vaccine helps to stop the body being infected with a particular microorganism and prevents a particular disease. It contains dead or weakened microorganisms or the poisons they make. The vaccine is injected into the body. The immune system makes antibodies against the microorganism which can stay in the body for many years and kill any live microorganism of that type that enter it. This then makes the body immune to the disease.

❚ Vaccination is the best way of preventing the spread of infectious disease.

INVESTIGATE
Find out what diseases you have been immunised against.

The danger of drugs

Prescription drugs such as antibiotics are used to fight disease, but there are other drugs that are harmful to the body. They damage the organs of the body and are addictive. This means they make the person want more and more of the drug. The bodies of addicted people may become so damaged that eventually their organs fail to work and they die.

CIGARETTES

The tobacco in cigarettes contains the addictive drug nicotine. Tobacco also contains substances such as tar that can cause the body's cells to change. When that happens, the cell's nucleus loses control and the cell becomes a cancer cell. Over time a group of cancer cells called a tumour may develop in the mouth, throat or lungs. Tumours can prove fatal. Smoking can also damage the circulatory system, leading to heart attacks or strokes, and attacks the lungs, causing respiratory illnesses such as emphysema.

▌Cigarette smoke contains many harmful substances. Even breathing someone else's cigarette smoke (passive smoking) is bad for your health.

ALCOHOL

All alcoholic drinks contain the drug alcohol. Alcohol is poisonous, but when it enters the body the liver cells break it down to make it harmless. If a person drinks alcohol faster than their liver can work, the alcohol affects the nervous system and makes them drunk. A drunk person thinks more slowly and has less control over how they move. This makes them more likely to have an accident and injure themselves. They can also become violent or reckless and their actions can harm others. In time, people who drink large amounts of alcohol may suffer irreversible liver damage which can prove fatal.

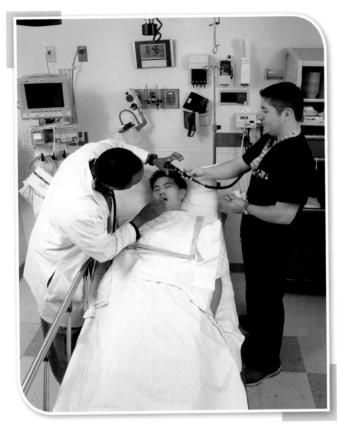

▌ People who take dangerous drugs often need emergency medical treatment.

ILLEGAL DRUGS

Illegal drugs include cannabis, cocaine, heroin, ecstasy and amphetamines. They all affect the way nerve cells in the nervous system work and can change how people behave. They can affect other body systems too. Cannabis can make people see things that are not there. Cocaine, ecstasy and amphetamines make a person move about quickly and carelessly and become confused. This increases their chances of injuring themselves in an accident. Heroin slows down the working of nerve cells so much that the body can die. Addiction to any of them can be fatal.

INVESTIGATE

Find out more about the dangers of illegal drugs from the booklets and pamphlets that your school may have.

▌ Cannabis for sale. Smoking cannabis can make you confused, forgetful and anxious.

Exercise and health

Exercise keeps your body healthy. It makes many of the organ systems work together better. Scientists believe that you should take at least an hour of exercise every day. In that hour some time should be spent on gentle activities such as walking or slow cycling and some should be spent on more strenuous activities such as running, swimming or playing football.

❚ Swimming is a great way to exercise the muscles in your arms, chest and legs.

THE SKELETAL SYSTEM

Gentle exercise, such as walking and cycling, makes the bones and ligaments stronger. Ligaments hold the bones together in their joints so stronger ligaments produce stronger joints that are less likely to become damaged or sprained.

Sprinting builds up powerful leg muscles, a strong pumping heart and a fast-acting respiratory system.

THE MUSCULAR SYSTEM

Exercise works and strengthens the muscles. During exercise the respiration rate of the muscles increases to release energy for action. This means the muscles need more oxygen than at rest so they can work harder. At the same time the blood needs to get rid of the extra carbon dioxide that the muscles produce.

THE CIRCULATORY SYSTEM

The muscles in the heart pump the blood around the body (see pages 8–11.) During exercise, the heart must pump the blood faster so that all muscles get enough oxygen to work and excess carbon dioxide can be removed. As you exercise more, your heart becomes stronger and allows you to exercise for longer.

THE RESPIRATORY SYSTEM

The respiratory system is made up of the lungs, the ribs and their muscles and the diaphragm. These organs work together to let you breathe. When you breathe in, the rib muscles pull up the ribs, the diaphragm goes down and the lungs expand and take in air. When you breathe out the rib muscles relax, the ribs go down, the diaphragm comes up and the lungs become smaller and push air out. During exercise all these actions speed up to take in more oxygen, get rid of the extra carbon dioxide and allow you to exercise more strongly for longer.

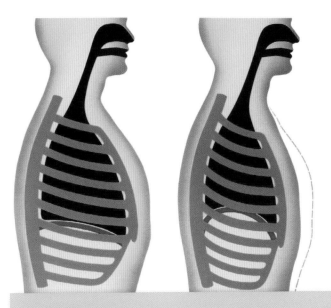

The diaphragm (red) goes up and down in the opposite direction to the ribs as you breathe in and out.

INVESTIGATE

How does your heartbeat change with exercise? Rest for a minute, then take your pulse. Exercise for two minutes, then take your pulse again. Do different types of exercise, such as walking and running, produce different results?

A healthy lifestyle

Everyone should have a healthy lifestyle. It helps all the organ systems of the body to work at their best. There are many simple activities you can do to keep your body healthy.

SLEEP

Sleep helps all the organ systems to rest after a busy day. This is particularly important for the brain as a lack of sleep makes it harder to learn and remember. Experts recommend that nine- to eleven-year-olds have between nine and ten hours' sleep each night.

❙ Too much time watching a screen can disrupt your sleep, so put your tablet away well before bedtime.

❙ Antibacterial soap kills any harmful microorganisms on your hands.

KEEPING CLEAN

Washing the skin regularly reduces the number of microorganisms living on it and reduces the chance of harmful ones entering a cut. Washing hands after visiting the toilet and before handling food also helps to reduce the chance of passing on infection.

DENTAL CARE

Teeth need to be cleaned twice a day. This removes a thin yellow film called plaque that builds up on them. Plaque is made by microorganisms feeding on food that coats the teeth. If plaque is allowed to build up, it turns to a hard substance called tartar which can cause gum disease. Brushing also removes acids that can damage the surface of the teeth and cause decay. You should visit the dentist twice a year to have your teeth checked for tartar build-up and signs of decay, as well as to see if they are growing properly.

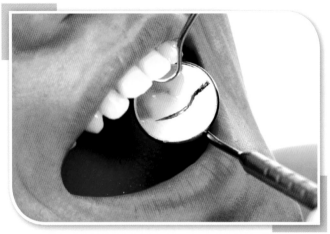

❙ This mirror allows the dentist to check the condition of the back of your teeth.

DIET

People need to eat a balanced diet that provides them with all the nutrients that their body needs (see p.18–19). They should also take care not to eat too many sweet or fatty foods that can lead to obesity. Many fizzy drinks contain large amounts of sugar (up to eight heaped teaspoons) and very few nutrients. They can damage teeth and increase the chances of someone becoming obese. Eating a lot of salt in the diet can lead to diseases of the circulatory system, so intake of salty snacks such as crisps should be reduced and replaced with healthier alternatives such as yoghurt and fruit.

❙ Hikes in the countryside with friends are a great way to exercise and have fun.

EXERCISE

Regular exercise has many benefits for the body (see pages 24–25). It also helps people to sleep well and to feel more alert and energetic. Everyone should make sure that they take part in some form of activity for at least an hour a day

INVESTIGATE

Check your lifestyle against the features described here. Is it healthy? If not, what could you do to improve it?

Investigating the body

People have been investigating how the body works for over two thousand years. Their discoveries still inform science and medicine today.

HIPPOCRATES (c.440–C.370 BCE)

Hippocrates was a Greek doctor. He examined people with many different illnesses and set out rules for their care. Hippocrates discovered that a person's health could be affected by their diet and lifestyle. Doctors today still take an oath named after him – the Hippocratic Oath – to follow his teachings and uphold his high medical standards of patient care.

GALEN (c.129–216 CE)

Galen was a Greek doctor who worked in the Roman Empire. He was interested in the structure of bodies and cut up animal bodies because he was not allowed to dissect human bodies at this time. His work helped to introduce people to the structure of bodies. Some of his ideas were later found to be wrong. For example, Galen believed that animal bodies were arranged just like human bodies and they are not. He was also convinced that blood moved up and down inside the body like the tide rising and falling on a seashore. Although these ideas were shown to be wrong, they did inspire others to make investigations and build up the science of medicine.

HIPPOCRATES HIRACLIDÆ F. COVS.
Ex marmore antiquo.

❙ Hippocrates observed his patients carefully to build up his knowledge of illnesses.

WILLIAM HARVEY (1578–1657)

Harvey was a British doctor who studied blood circulation in animals and began to experiment on humans. He did not think blood moved as Galen believed, and demonstrated by tying a cloth tightly around an arm that the blood only flowed one way through the blood vessels. He went on to claim that the heart propels the blood in one direction through the blood vessels so that it circulates around the body from the heart to the other organs of the body.

❙ Harvey's experiment on the arm showed that veins contained valves and that blood only flows one way through them.

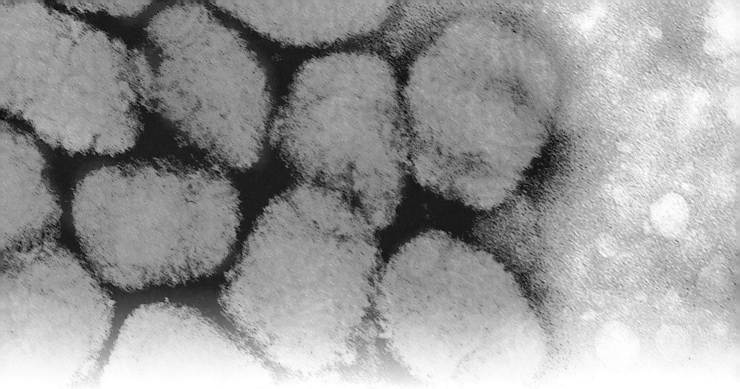

I A highly magnified image of the smallpox virus.

EDWARD JENNER (1749–1823)

Jenner was a British doctor who studied the immune system. He saw that some milkmaids caught a disease called cowpox from cattle. When the milkmaids recovered, he found they were immune to a more dangerous disease called smallpox. He tested this observation by vaccinating a boy with cowpox germs and then later with smallpox germs. The boy recovered from both infections. The vaccination had made the boy immune to smallpox. In 1853, the smallpox vaccine was made compulsory in the UK. Worldwide, there have been no cases of smallpox since 1977.

I Despite Jenner's vaccination being successful, people were distrustful of receiving germs from cows and this cartoon even shows Jenner's patients growing cows out of their bodies!

INVESTIGATE

Find out how the work of Louis Pasteur, Joseph Lister and Alexander Fleming has helped to save lives.

WILLIAM BEAUMONT (1785–1853)

Beaumont was a US surgeon. One of his patients had a bullet wound that had left a hole in his stomach. The patient allowed Beaumont to put food samples attached to string into his stomach, then remove them to see if the stomach juices digested them. Beaumont found that they did. His experiments showed digestive juices play a major part in breaking down food to release its nutrients.

Glossary

Atrium – a chamber or cavity in the top half of the heart which receives blood from other organs of the body.

Bacteria – a type of microorganism with a body made from a cell that does not have a nucleus.

Bicuspid – a valve with two flaps.

Bladder – a balloon-like organ in which urine is stored before it is released.

Blood vessel – a tube which carries blood such as an artery, capillary or vein.

Cell – a microscopic structure containing a nucleus and cytoplasm in which all life processes take place. Cells join together in huge numbers to make up the organs of the body.

Cowpox – a viral infection which affects cows.

Cytoplasm – a jelly-like substance in a cell where processes which keep the cell alive take place.

Decay – to break up or rot due to the action of microorganisms.

Diaphragm – a sheet of muscle which runs across the body below the ribs. Its movements help in breathing.

Dissect – to cut up.

DNA – the letters stand for deoxyribonucleic acid. This contains all the instructions for how a cell works and information that can be passed from one generation to another during reproduction.

Emphysema – a disease of the lungs where the lung surface is severely damaged.

Enzyme – a chemical substance made in the body that can make changes in other substances without being changed itself.

Fibre (general) – a long, thin structure.

Fibre (in digestion) – a material found in cereals, bread and potatoes that is not digested but passes through the digestive system, helping the muscles in the tube walls to push food along.

Fungi – living things which produce spores in order to reproduce. Some fungi, such as yeast, stay as single cells during their whole life cycle.

Haemoglobin – the red substance in red blood cells. When it joins with oxygen, it forms oxyhaemogloin which is brighter red.

Immune – protected against a particular disease.

Invertebrates – animals that do not have a backbone or skeleton of bone or cartilage.

Microorganism – living things which can only be seen with the aid of a microscope.

Microscope – a scientific instrument that is used to give highly magnified views of objects.

Nucleus – the part of a cell which controls all of its activities.

Nutrient – a substance found in foods that the body needs to help it grow and stay alive.

Obesity – a condition in which the body contains large amounts of fat, making it unhealthily overweight.

Organ – a part of the body which performs a particular task in keeping the body alive such as pumping blood (the heart) or digesting and absorbing food (small intestine). Organs join together to create organ systems.

Photosynthesis – the process by which plants made food in their leaves using sunlight, carbon dioxide and water.

Protoctista – living things made from one cell that contains a nucleus.

Pulse – the expansion and contraction of an artery due to the action of the heart.

Respiration – a process in the body in which energy is released from food to keep the body alive.

Smallpox – a very infectious viral disease that causes a high fever and a rash with red sores.

Spinal cord – a cord made of many nerve cells running down the back inside the backbone.

Stethoscope – a medical instrument used to listen to the sounds made by the heart or by the lungs.

Stroke – a condition that develops in the body if the blood flow to the brain is reduced and brain cells die. This in turn prevents the nervous system from working properly.

Tissue – a group of similar cells which perform a task in the life of the body.

Tricuspid – a valve with three flaps.

Tumour – a mass of diseased cells.

Vaccinate – to inject someone with a vaccine.

Vaccine – an injection which contains dead or weakened microbes of a particular disease which protects someone against that disease.

Vena cava – a vein which brings blood from the body to the right atrium of the heart.

Ventricle – a chamber or cavity in the bottom half of the heart which pumps blood away from the heart in arteries.

Vertebrates – animals with a backbone. They have a skeleton of bone or cartilage.

Urea – a waste product formed when proteins break down. It usually passes out of the body in the urine.

Urine – a watery liquid containing urea and other wastes from the cells.

Windpipe – the tube which connects the mouth to the lungs.

Index

ABOUT THIS BOOK

The aim of this book is provide information and enrichment for the topic of the Human Body in the Upper Key Stage 2 UK Science Curriculum. There are five lines of scientific enquiry. By reading the book the children are making one of them – research using secondary sources. They are encouraged to make more on pages 13, 15, 17, 21, 23, 29. There are other lines of enquiry to be made on the following pages - Observing over time: pages 5, 11, 19, 25; Pattern-seeking: page 25; Making a comparative or fair test: pages 19, 25, 27. There are many other skills to be developed in science and the following pages give opportunities to develop some of them: Model-making page 7, 9; Performing a measurement and calculation: page 15; Drawing a conclusion: page 19.